THE BEST
DOGS
EVER

NEWFOUNDLANDS ARE THE BEST!

Elaine Landau

LERNER PUBLICATIONS COMPANY · MINNEAPOLIS

To Marge Cox

Lerner Publications Company
A division of Lerner Publishing Group, Inc.
241 First Avenue North
Minneapolis, MN 55401 U.S.A.

Website address: www.lernerbooks.com

Library of Congress Cataloging-in-Publication Data

Landau, Elaine.
    Newfoundlands are the best! / by Elaine Landau.
        p.   cm. – (The best dogs ever)
    Includes index.
    ISBN 978-0-7613-6082-7 (lib. bdg. : alk. paper)
    1. Newfoundland dog—Juvenile literature. I. Title.
  SF429.N4L36 2011
  636.73—dc22   2010023129

Manufactured in the United States of America
1 — CG — 12/31/10

TABLE OF CONTENTS

25.26

CHAPTER ONE
WHAT A PAL!

What do you look for in a friend? How about someone who's fun to be with? Would you also want a friend who's loyal, smart, and kind?

If so, I have a pal you might like. It's not a person, though. It's a super dog known as a Newfoundland, or Newf for short.

One Huge Pooch

The Newf is not a tiny pooch. You won't be carrying this dog around in your backpack. Male adult dogs stand about 28 inches (71 centimeters) high at the shoulder. They can weigh as much as 150 pounds (68 kilograms). Female dogs are a little smaller.

THE BEST NAME EVER

Give your Newf a name it can proudly answer to. Do any of these fit your wonderful woofer?

Hercules

Beefy   VENUS

Titan   Goliath

Xena

Athena   Wookie

Neptune   JUMBO

Not Hard on the Eyes

Newfs are great-looking pooches. These big-boned beauties have large heads and broad backs. They have thick, furry double coats too.

DID YOU KNOW?

Dogs with double coats have two layers of fur. One layer is short and lies close to the dog's skin. The other layer is long and grows over the shorter layer.

Newfs come in different colors. They may be solid black, brown, or gray. At times, these dogs may have white on their chins, chests, toes, and tail tips. Other Newfs are known as Landseers. These dogs are mostly white with black markings.

This Newf is a Landseer—a white Newf with black markings.

A Great Big Bundle of Love

Newfs are not only attractive. They are also very sweet. They are among the most caring and gentle dogs around.

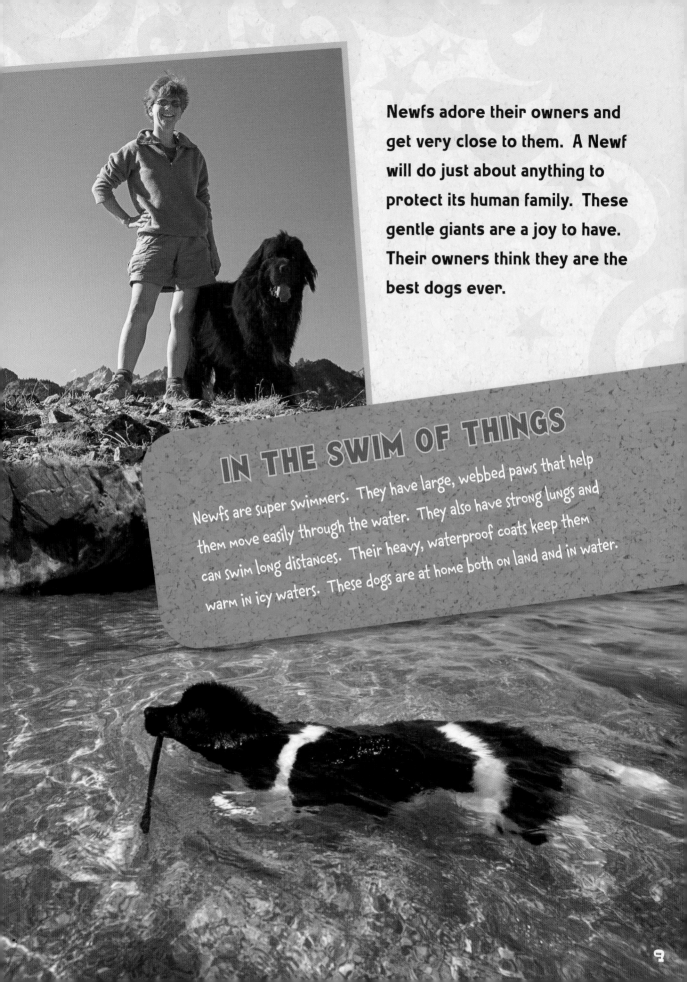

Newfs adore their owners and get very close to them. A Newf will do just about anything to protect its human family. These gentle giants are a joy to have. Their owners think they are the best dogs ever.

IN THE SWIM OF THINGS

Newfs are super swimmers. They have large, webbed paws that help them move easily through the water. They also have strong lungs and can swim long distances. Their heavy, waterproof coats keep them warm in icy waters. These dogs are at home both on land and in water.

CHAPTER TWO
AT THE START

People have told many stories about Newfs. Some of these stories say the dogs came to North America on Viking ships.

A Viking ship sails the sea in the early eleventh century.

Is this true? No one knows for sure. But we do know that Newfs later became quite popular in the United States. George Washington had two Newfs. Statesman and scientist Ben Franklin had a Newf as well.

George Washington (upper left) and Ben Franklin (above) both enjoyed having Newfs as pets.

An Island Pooch

Newfs got their start in Newfoundland, Canada. Farmers there used them to haul carts of farm goods and firewood. Newfs also helped deliver the mail by pulling mail carts. Fishers used Newfs to haul in fishing nets. These dogs put in long hours. They were hardworking pooches.

This Newf is pulling a large cart. Newfs in Canada once pulled carts for farmers and mail carriers.

A Newf befriends a Canadian soldier in 1917.

Yet in time, Newfs became more than working dogs. People saw that these gentle, loving canines made great companions. They became much-loved pets.

BEST IN SHOW

A Newf named Darbydale's All Rise Pouch Cove (*above*) was the 2004 Westminster champion.

WINNING NEWFS

Newfs are prize-winning pooches. These dogs have twice won Best in Show at the Westminster Kennel Club Dog Show. In 1984, a black Newf named Seaward's Blackbeard took the prize. This darling dog was in super shape. His handler walked him 3 miles (5 kilometers) daily.

In 2004, Darbydale's All Rise Pouch Cove won. The day this champion took the title, he seemed to know he was great looking. He strutted around the show ring with pride.

Basset hounds are part of the hound group.

Part of a Great Group of Dogs

The American Kennel Club (AKC) groups dogs by breed. Some of the AKC's groups include the toy group, the sporting group, and the hound group.

Springer spaniels, like this one, are in the sporting group.

Yorkshire terriers are part of the toy group.

Newfs are in the working group. Dogs in the working group are large, smart, and strong. They are quick learners too.

HUGE HELPERS

Newfs have long been super search and rescue dogs. During World War II (1939–1945), Newfs served the United States well. When a plane went down in the wilderness, these dogs helped find the aircraft and crew. The dogs also did water rescues. Newfs are still used for search and rescue missions.

A Newf practices water rescues by pulling a life preserver to shore.

CHAPTER THREE

THE RIGHT DOG FOR YOU?

Sweet, fun, and furry. That's a Newf all right.
Who wouldn't want a dog like that?

You may think that a Newf is the perfect pet for you. But don't rush out to get one just yet. Read on to see if this breed is really a good match for your family.

Newfs are friendly dogs—but is a Newfoundland right for you?

Do You Really Want a Huge Pet?

Giant dogs need lots of space. They need room outside to exercise and play. Do you live in a small apartment? Or a house without yard? If so, think twice before getting a Newf.

A HIGH-PRICED POOCH

Newfs are purebred dogs. They can be quite costly. Some breeders charge more than $1,000 for a pup. Can you afford a high-priced pet? Talk this over with your family.

Newfs need plenty of space to run.

Oh Dear! What Have We Here?

There's no getting around it: Newfs drool and slobber.
When they shake their heads, the saliva
flies. Some people think it's cute.
Others see it as a wet mess.
How do you feel about
drool and slobber?

RESCUE NEWFS

Some families adopt older Newfs instead of puppies. Full-grown Newfs can be found at rescue centers for this breed. Rescue Newfs are usually a bit cheaper than Newf pups. But families who adopt them still must pay for health care, food, and pet supplies.

Hair Everywhere

Newfs shed a lot. Expect dog hair everywhere. But don't expect your family to hire a maid to clean up after your pooch. If you get a Newf, you'll be doing a lot of vacuuming. Get used to the idea.

Big dogs can be a handful. This Newf is so tall that it can reach the kitchen sink!

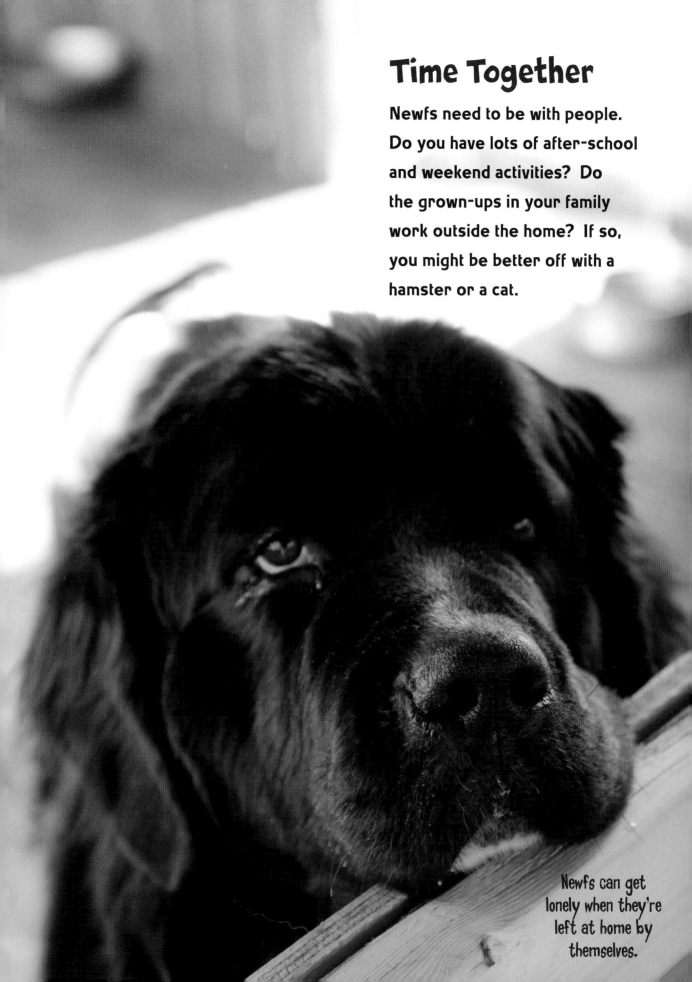

Time Together

Newfs need to be with people. Do you have lots of after-school and weekend activities? Do the grown-ups in your family work outside the home? If so, you might be better off with a hamster or a cat.

Newfs can get lonely when they're left at home by themselves.

Have you decided if a Newf is right for you? If it is, you've picked one of the best-natured breeds around. Get ready to welcome an oversized canine cutie to your home.

Newfs make wonderful pals.

CHAPTER FOUR

WELCOMING YOUR WOOFER

The day you've waited for is here. You're getting your Newf! You couldn't be happier or more excited.

Be Prepared

You'll want your dog to feel at home right away. Not sure what you'll need to welcome Fido to your family? This basic list is a great place to start.

- collar
- leash
- tags (for identification)
- dog food
- food and water bowls
- crates (one for when your pet travels by car and one for it to rest in at home)
- treats (to be used in training)
- toys

Visit Your Vet

Take your Newf to a veterinarian as soon as possible. That's a doctor who treats animals. They are called vets for short.

The vet will check your dog's health. Your pooch will also get the shots it needs. Take your Newf back to the vet for regular checkups. Also take your dog to the vet if it becomes ill.

START TRAINING EARLY

Training is important with any large dog. A giant pooch can easily knock over a small child without meaning to. You'll need to teach your Newf not to jump up on people. Fortunately, Newfs are very smart. That makes them fast learners and easy to train.

Feeding Time

Ask your vet what to feed your dog. Dogs need different food at different stages of their lives. Don't feed your dog table scraps. Otherwise, you may end up with a pudgy pooch.

USE TREATS FOR TRAINING

Don't give your Newf doggie treats for a snack or dessert. Use them as rewards in training. Give your Newf a treat when it obeys a command.

Coat Care

Newfs have thick, beautiful coats. It's best to brush your dog daily. This will keep its skin and coat in tip-top shape.

In addition to brushing, you'll need to bathe your Newf.

You and Your Newf

Your Newf will be your BFF (best friend forever).
So give your dog the life it deserves. Make it
feel like part of your family. Pet and play with
your pooch even when you're busy or tired.
You'll be glad you did. In return, you'll get
loads of love from your huge, furry pal.

Glossary

American Kennel Club (AKC): an organization that groups dogs by breed. The AKC also defines the characteristics of different breeds.

breed: a particular type of dog. Dogs of the same breed have the same body shape and general features.

breeder: someone who mates dogs to produce a particular type of dog

canine: a dog, or having to do with dogs

coat: a dog's fur

Landseer: a Newfoundland whose coat is mostly white with black markings

purebred: a dog whose parents are of the same breed

rescue center: a shelter where stray and abandoned dogs are kept until they are adopted

search and rescue dog: a dog that finds people after disasters

shed: to lose fur

veterinarian: a doctor who treats animals. Veterinarians are called vets for short.

webbed: connected by a web or fold of skin

working group: a group of dogs that were bred to do different types of jobs, such as guarding property, carrying messages, or pulling sleds

For More Information

Books

Brecke, Nicole, and Patricia M. Stockland. *Dogs You Can Draw*. Minneapolis: Millbrook Press, 2010. Perfect for dog lovers, this colorful book teaches readers how to draw many different popular dog breeds.

Landau, Elaine. *Your Pet Dog*. Rev. ed. New York: Children's Press, 2007. This title is a good guide for young people on choosing and caring for a dog.

O'Sullivan, Robyn. *More Than Man's Best Friend: The Story of Working Dogs*. Washington, DC: National Geographic, 2006. This book features profiles of various working dogs. Readers will enjoy learning about these clever canines and the tasks they perform.

Wheeler, Jill C. *Newfoundlands*. Edina, MN: Abdo, 2010. This easy-to-read text describes the history and habits of the Newfoundland. It also provides information on caring for the Newfoundland.

Websites

American Kennel Club

http://www.akc.org

Visit this website to find a complete listing of AKC-registered dog breeds, including the Newfoundland. The site also features fun printable activities for kids.

FBI Working Dogs

http://www.fbi.gov/kids/dogs/doghome.htm

This fun site explains all about working dogs and tells how canine crime fighters help the FBI.

LERNER *e* SOURCE™

Expand learning beyond the printed book. Download free, complementary educational resources for this book from our website, www.lernerresource.com

Index

Photo Acknowledgments

The images in this book are used with the permission of: backgrounds © iStockphoto.com/Julie Fisher and © iStockphoto.com/Tomasz Adamczyk; © iStockphoto.com/Michael Balderas, p. 1; © Cynoclub/Dreamstime.com, pp. 4 (right), 7 (right); © Eric Isselée/Dreamstime.com, pp. 4 (left), 14 (right); © iStockphoto.com/Cynoclub, p. 5; © EML/Shutterstock Images, p. 6; © Martin Harvey/Digital Vision/Getty Images, pp. 7 (left), 17 (top), 26 (left); © Hadas Dembo/Taxi/Getty Images, p. 8; © age fotostock/SuperStock, p. 9 (top); © NaturePL/SuperStock, pp. 9 (bottom), 18 (bottom); The Granger Collection, New York, p. 10; © SuperStock/SuperStock, p. 11 (top left, and right); © Mary Evans Picture Library/The Image Works, p. 11 (bottom left); © All Canada Photos/SuperStock, p. 12 (top); © katewarn images/Alamy, p. 12 (bottom); © Stephen Chernin/Getty Images, p. 13 (left); © Topical Press Agency/Hulton Archive/Getty Images, p. 13 (right); © Jszg005/Dreamstime.com, p. 14 (left); © Jerry Shulman/SuperStock, pp. 14-15; © Jean-Luc & Françoise Ziegler/Bios/ Photolibrary, p. 15; © Juniors Bildarchiv/Alamy, p. 16; © H. Mark Weidman Photography/Alamy, p. 17 (bottom); © Gerard Brown/Dorling Kindersley/Getty Images, p. 18 (top); © Froggy/Dreamstime. com, p. 19; © DEA/C. SAPPA/De Agostini Picture Library/Getty Images, p. 20 (top); AP Photo/ The Forum, Dave Wallis, p. 20 (bottom); © Isabel Poulin/Dreamstime.com, p. 21; © Science Faction/ SuperStock, p. 22 (left); © shapencolour/Alamy, p. 22 (right); © Fancy/Alamy, p. 23; © Tammy Mcallister/Dreamstime.com, p. 24 (top); © April Turner/Dreamstime.com, p. 24 (second from top); © iStockphoto.com/orix3, p. 24 (second from bottom); © Martin Harvey/Workbook Stock/Getty Images, p. 24 (bottom); © Waldemar Dabrowski/Dreamstime.com, p. 25; © Jose Manuel Gelpi Diaz/ Dreamstime.com, p. 26 (right); © Loflo69/Dreamstime.com, p. 27 (top left); © 1Apix/Alamy, p. 27 (top right); © iStockphoto.com/Michael Balderas, p. 27 (bottom); AP Photo/Frank Franklin II, p. 28 (top); © Shannon Stapleton/Reuters/CORBIS, p. 28 (bottom); © Ariel Skelley/Riser/Getty Images, p. 29.

Front and Back Cover: © Eric Isselée/Dreamtime.com.